LOOKING for CRABS

To Rosie for her inspiration
and constant support

AN ANGUS & ROBERTSON BOOK
An imprint of HarperCollinsPublishers

First published in 1992 by
CollinsAngus&Robertson Publishers Pty Limited (ACN 009 913 517)
A division of HarperCollinsPublishers (Australia) Pty Limited
25-31 Ryde Road, Pymble NSW 2073, Australia

HarperCollinsPublishers (New Zealand) Limited
31 View Road, Glenfield, Auckland 10, New Zealand

HarperCollinsPublishers Limited
77- 85 Fulham Palace Road, London W6 8JB, United Kingdom

Distributed in the United States of America by
HarperCollinsPublishers
10 East 53rd Street, New York NY 10022, USA

National Library of Australia
Cataloguing-in-Publication data:

Whatley, Bruce.
  Looking for crabs

  ISBN 0 207 17596 9.

  1. Crabs - Juvenile literature, I Title.
595.3842

Printed in Hong Kong

5 4 3 2 1
96 95 94 93 92

LOOKING for CRABS

BRUCE WHATLEY

Angus&Robertson
An imprint of HarperCollinsPublishers

I love going to the beach for holidays.
Sometimes it's too cold to swim
so we go looking for crabs.

Rock pools are a great place
to look for crabs,
but you have to be very quiet.

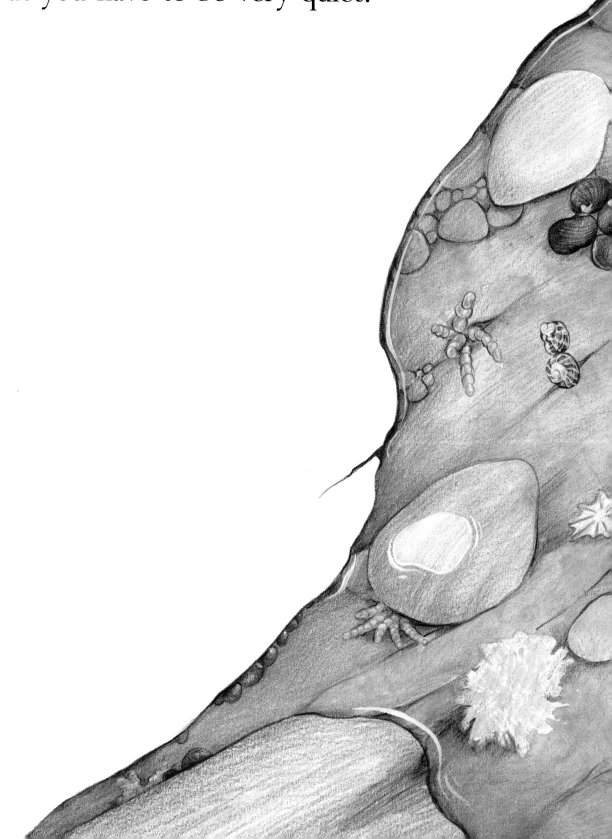

Crabs can be difficult to find.
You have to look really hard,
but try not to scare them!

Dad says crabs are usually found
under little rocks
at the bottom of rock pools.

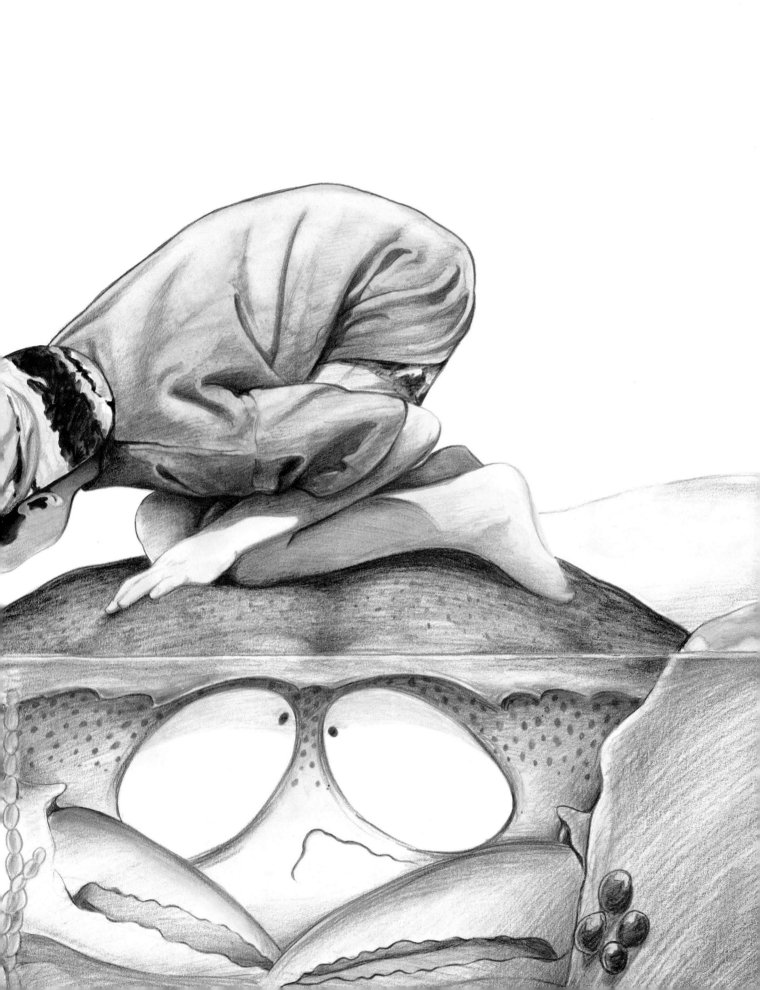

Mum says you have to tread carefully so you don't hurt them.

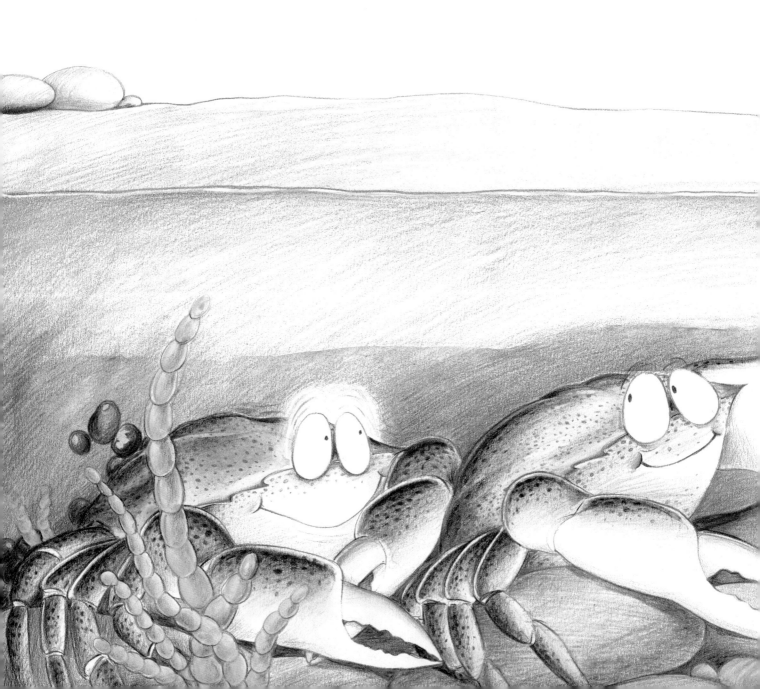

But I don't think there can be
any crabs at our beach.

Even when Dad lifted up
a really big rock
we didn't find any.

Mum said they were probably out to lunch,
but I think they were just hiding.

Crabs are very good at hiding.
I couldn't see any in my little pool.

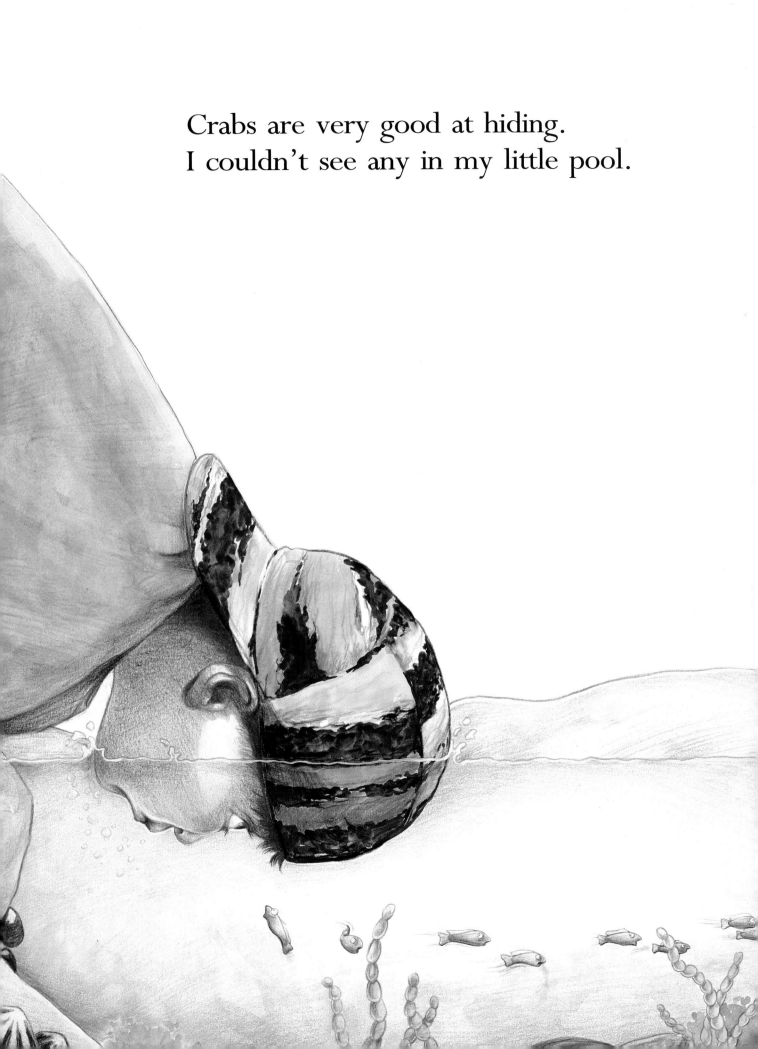

Sometimes you find hermit crabs
living in little shells.
But not when we were on holiday.

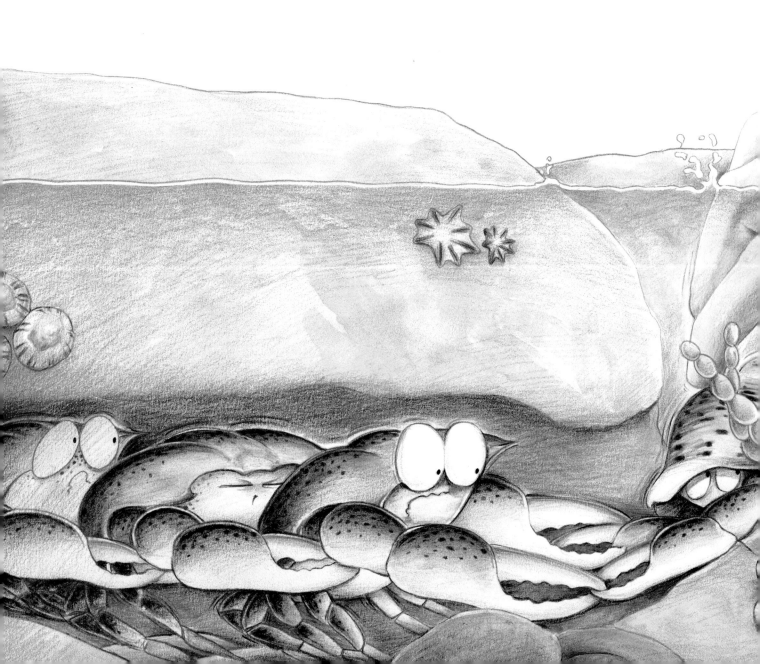

Where do they go in the holidays?
Dad suggested Hawaii.

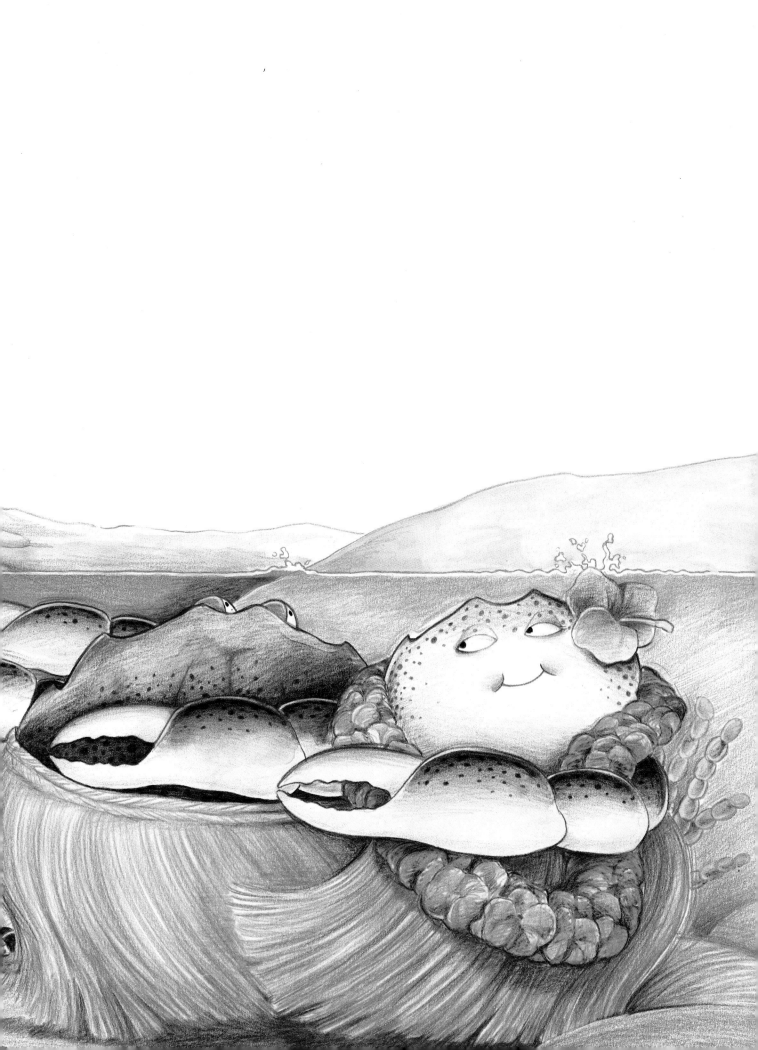

My little sister said Disneyland.
I told them we just weren't
looking hard enough.

I don't know where the crabs go
in the holidays.
But one thing I do know . . .

There are no crabs at our beach!

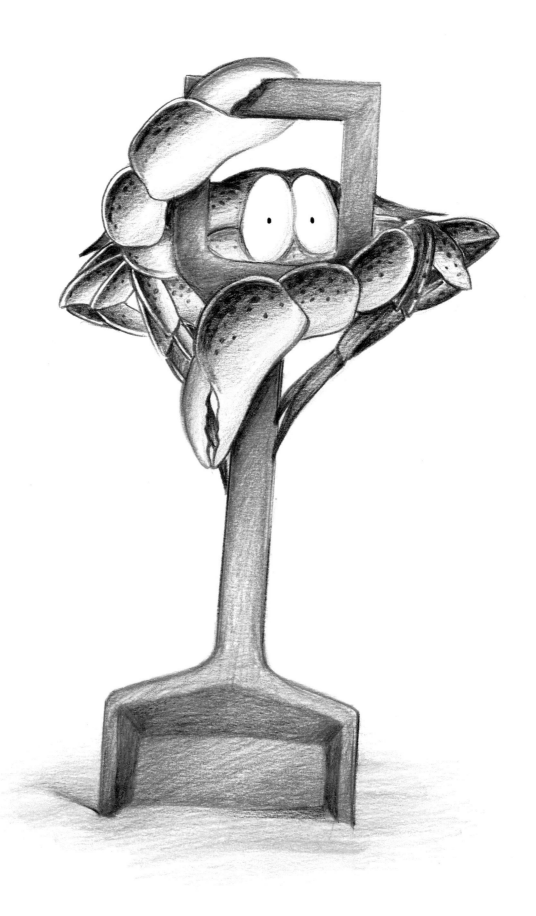